THE MANUSCRIPT 12-STAVE WORKBOOK

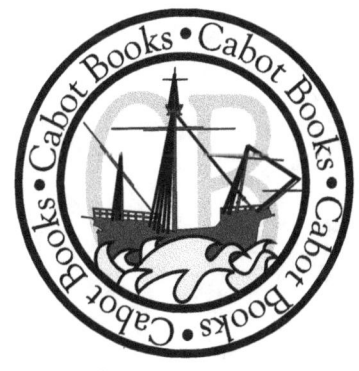

A Fretted Friends Publication for Cabot Books

Published by:
Cabot Books
Copyright © 2016 by Cabot Books
All rights reserved.

First Edition April 2016

ISBN-13: 978-1-906207-94-6

No part of this publication may be reproduced in any form
or by any means without the prior consent of the publisher.

Cabot Books
3 Kenton Mews
Henleaze
Bristol
BS9 4LT
United Kingdom

Visit our online site at www.frettedfriendsmusic.com
e-mail: cabotbooks@blueyonder.co.uk